Simple Jason Youn's ~~99¢~~ Photography Guide

By: Jason Youn

2nd Edition

DSLR
Digital Single Lens Reflex
*A DSLR camera has a **Digital** image sensor like a CCD or CMOS instead of film. It has a **Single Lens** that light passes through, either on its way to your eyepiece or your image sensor. A **Reflex** camera allows the photographer to simultaneously view and focus the image that is to be captured.*

For Elle & Juliet

ISBN-13:
978-1491231128

ISBN-10:
1491231122

For licensing and reproduction permission contact information visit www.JasonYoun.com. For academic use bulk pricing is available.

Author: Jason Youn
Editor: Ramona Howard

This is the print version of the
best selling Kindle classic:

Jason Youn's 99¢ Photography Guide

Obviously we cannot afford to create and sell a
paperback book for less than a buck,
hence the higher price :)

Table Of Contents
--*-*-*-*-*

Chapter 1

Introduction

Summer was here, and our family was off to see the Grand Canyon. As we prepared to embark on our road trip, my dad purchased a pair of matching plastic 110 format point and shoot cameras, one for my brother Andrew, and the other one for me. We would spend hours of our trip taking pictures of just about anything. Our favorite game was to see if we could make a photograph of each other at the exact same moment so that we could capture the other camera's flash on film. This effort did not produce the special effect we had hoped. Actually it proved itself impossible, and we ended up with two spent rolls of really bad pictures. From looking over our developed photographs you would never guess that we actually went to the Grand Canyon. For the most part, our photos were of the inside of pockets, a random squirrel as it ran past, or each other as we worked for our illusive simultaneous flash shot. As the years past, I continued to waste time and film making really bad photographs; each one seemed worse than the one before, but it was still fun, and I was still shooting.

Soon I would discover the moving picture. With my parents' old Hi8 camera in hand, my friends and I set out to create a cinematic reproduction of Jules Verne's, *A Journey to the Center of the Earth*. After hours of work, a few pounds of gunpowder extracted from a model rocket kit, and the occasional feeling of panic as we searched for the fire extinguisher, our film was done. Once again, special effects would not make up for really bad camera work. The project was shelved and never seen again.

I would take my first photography class in high school. This time I had with me a simple SLR that shot 35mm film. Though the instructor tried to teach her pupils the finer points of black and white photography, it really did not help me all that much. In addition, the textbooks were not very good. They were filled with complex information, and at 300 some odd pages, they were too long to be useful to a beginner, or probably anyone for that matter. Although that class and textbook nearly killed it, my love of photography and cinematography remained strong and I sought richer waters.

College offered an ocean. I attended film school to learn how to become a movie maker. Though I studied motion picture and cinematography, my learning expanded beyond video; I actually learned more about still photography at that school than at any other single place. For the first time in my life the complexities of it all began to fit together. The relationships between ISO, aperture, shutter speed, and lighting came into focus -- and so did my images.

After a brief stint in television, I decided the industry was not for me and I went back to school to earn a degree in Art History with a minor in Religious Studies from ASU. I kept working with still photography.

Soon my work got some attention, won some awards, and people began to hire me to do everything from weddings and portraits, to sports, catalogue, and product shots. I began doing art shows and selling my landscape work; in short, photography was finally working for me.

I found that I was good at instructing people on how to use their own shiny new cameras. All those numbers and settings mean something, and if you can learn how and why to use them, you will be a better photographer. Beyond that there are some simple rules of art that humanity has spend the last 3,000 years or so mastering. I didn't invent these rules but I can tell you what they are, and if you can keep them in your mind as you shoot, you will be a better photographer. This is why I embarked upon this book. Anyone can take a picture. To create a photograph requires just little bit of information and a good deal of practice.

The Camera

The word camera comes from the Latin phrase, *Camera Obscura*, meaning "a dark chamber." Add a small hole to that chamber and light can enter into it at one place. So that the light can be focused, a lens is then added over the hole. One like this was mentioned in a book of optics dating back to the early 9th century A.D. Later, in the Renaissance period of Europe, these were used to help painters see how a 3D world might look when projected on a 2D plane such as a painting. Though this technology is at least 1200 years old, the basic principles still apply; and the physics of how a camera works closely match the human eye.

Cameras are like a man-made version of our eye. Light reflected off of objects enters the camera, or our eye, through a small hole with a lens; that light is then focused on the back wall of the camera or eye. A surface that is sensitive to light, and sometimes color, collects and records that image. This image of the outside world is projected upside down in the camera or eye. Our brains then take this upside down information and invert it for us so that we interpret the world with relative accuracy. In a camera we correct for the upside down image by rotating the print.

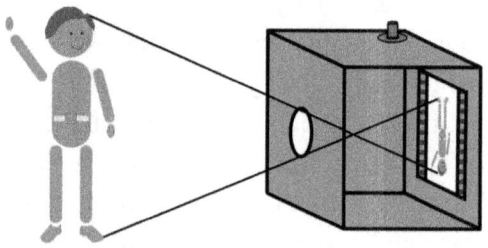

In 1826, Joseph Nicéphore Niépce created the first photograph when he discovered that a mixture of silver and chalk suspended in solution tended to darken on the side of its clear glass container that was exposed to sunlight. He took this solution and coated a piece of bitumen (a rock) and placed that in a *camera obscura*. Over the next eight hours, the camera collected light and focused that light on the silver coated bitumen. The first photograph, "View from the Window at Le Gras," was created.

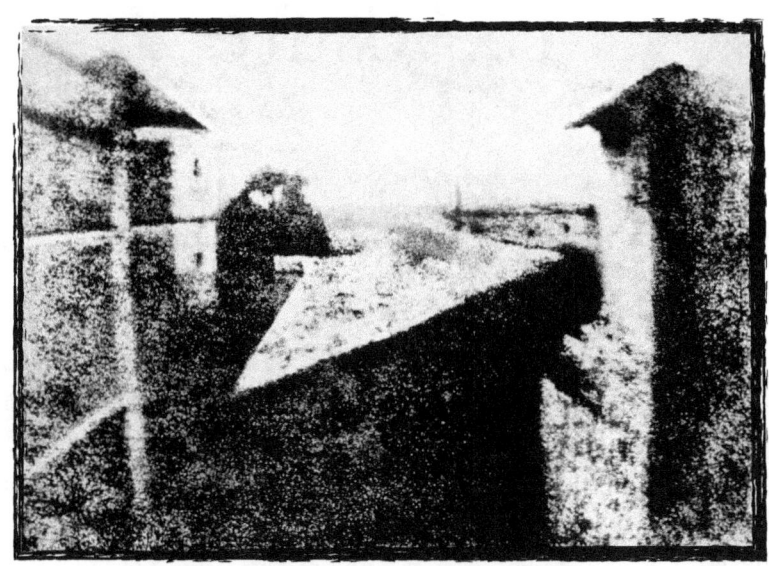

Joseph Nicéphore Niépce, "View from the Window at Le Gras," Silver on Bitumen - 1826

Cameras collect and then record light on a light sensitive surface. For nearly 100 years, film was the undisputed king of that world. Recently, however, it has been replaced by digital light collectors like CCD (charge-coupled device) or CMOS (complementary metal-oxide semiconductor) sensors. These new digital image sensors allow freedoms that normal film never could. The power to instantly review our images means that we can learn from our mistakes right away, rather than having to wait for a lab to develop our photographs and then tediously compare those images to our notes. Digital also means that we are no longer paying per image, so we can shoot a lot more without spending a lot more. Also ditching film means no longer having to work with those toxic lab chemicals. For all their differences however, the principals of film and digital photography are almost identical, and if you can shoot one, you can shoot the other.

Niepce's early camera had almost no way to control the amount of light it was taking in. He simply opened the shutter, and eight hours later he closed it. Our modern cameras have several ways to control the amount of light they collect and record. This is called exposure control.

Exposure

All cameras, film or digital, still or motion picture, have one simple thing in common. They all collect and record light. If you are taking a photograph of an object, the light that a camera collects starts at a light source like the sun or a lightbulb. The light then bounces off of an object, passes through the camera's lens and is focused onto a light sensitive material at the back of the camera, where it is recorded. (Though this light sensitive material can be a number of different things, for this book, we will call that material an image sensor; if you are shooting digital, this is what you are using.)

Exposure is the amount of light that comes through the lens and is collected by the image sensor. Proper exposure happens when enough light hits the image sensor to create an image that has light, dark, and middle tones.

TTL

Your camera can use auto exposure or manual exposure. Either way your camera has a built-in light meter that measures the amount of light being collected, and then either chooses the correct camera settings or informs you that your image is either underexposed (too dark), overexposed (too light), or properly exposed. Your camera collects this light through its lens, hence the name *Through The Lens* metering or *TTL*. If your camera is set to automatic, metering and exposure are done automatically. If your camera is set to manual, you will have to tell the camera what to do, but your camera will tell you how much light it has using its built-in TTL light meter. It will display this information with a line graph that looks something like the next image. Proper exposure will be in the middle of the graph, underexposed will be to the left and overexposed will be to right. For the details about how this looks on your specific camera, consult your owner's manual; most of the time, these indicators are obvious and can be found both on the camera's LCD screen located by the shutter release button, and in the digital readout found inside the reticle at the bottom of the frame. Here are three examples of how your light meter may look in a Canon camera. Nikon will look similar; other brands may vary.

Most of the time shooting with auto exposure is a good thing. It's fast, convenient, and simple to use, but there are some things that can cause your camera to become confused. In-camera light metering is based off a tone on the grey scale known as middle

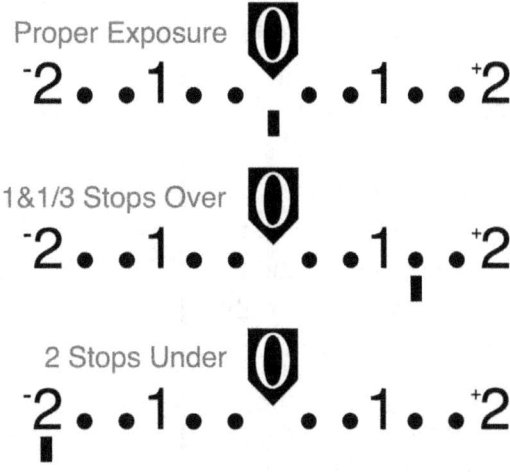

gray. The percent of light that is reflected off of middle gray is known and easily measurable. In a black and white photograph, a normal blue sky, the green leaves of a tree, and Anglo-Saxon skin all look to be just about middle gray when properly exposed. When the subject, or background, of your photograph are much darker or lighter than middle gray, your camera will get confused and your image will end up under or overexposed. For example if you are photographing a black dog, your camera may decide to overexpose the shot. Or if you are photographing on a ski slope surrounded by snow, your camera may decide to underexpose the image. If this is happening, you can easily correct for it with the exposure bias setting.

To find out how to adjust this on your camera, consult your owners manual. On my camera, you would press the shutter release button half way down, so the camera can meter the scene. Then you would turn a dial to tell the camera how much you would like it adjust its exposure bias, either over or underexposing the image, to compensate for your environment.

Histogram

If you shoot with a digital SLR, your camera can display a histogram. This histogram is like a bar graph; the dark parts of the image are represented on the left with the light parts on the right. If you have a lot of blacks, there will be a peak on the dark (left) side. If you have a lot of whites, there will be a peak on light (right) side. Normally, a properly exposed image has a histogram that looks much like a bell curve. If an image is heavy on the left there is a good chance that it is underexposed, and if is the heavy on the right there is a good chance that it is overexposed. The histogram works on a scale 0-255; zero equals black and 255 is equal to white. The following diagram shows three histograms: under-, well-, and overexposed.

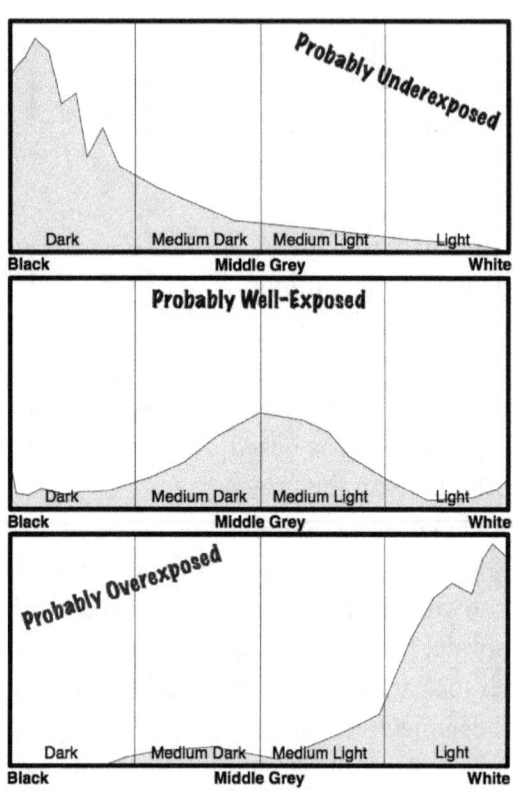

Stops

Stops are simply a way of measuring amounts of light. The scale functions by either halving or doubling the amount of light that makes it to the sensor. If an image is one stop overexposed, that means you have twice the amount of light required to create your image. If an image is one stop underexposed, that means you have half the amount of light required to create your image.

For the math people out there: You may have noticed that a scale based on doubles and halves is not linear like a ruler or measuring tape. Rather, it grows at a compounded rate, 1, 2, 4, 8, 16, 32, 64 and so on. This is because the scale is based on how our eyes perceive light. When there is a little bit of light in the room, our eye can see minor changes. When it's bright outside, it will take a much larger change for us to notice a difference in the lighting. So rather than the scale working with simply adding another unit of light, the light must either double or half each time in order for our eyes and brain to perceive a linear transition from one level to the next.

There are four ways to control the exposure of your image: *available light, aperture, shutter speed, & ISO.*

Available or Ambient light

Available light is light that is either already present -- *ambient* -- or can be added to your environment. You can add light many ways. Opening up the mini-blinds works. Artificial lighting, like the lights in the room, or a flash on the camera, will add light. Too much light will overexpose your image; Too little light will underexpose your image. For now, let's assume that our available light is a constant that cannot be controlled or changed. Later we will talk about how to control this with flashes, reflectors, and light bulbs.

For any given amount of light there are three ways to control your exposure, and all three of them are done right in your camera. Knowing how to control your aperture, shutter speed and ISO, is the foundation for knowing how to take your camera beyond fully automatic mode.

Aperture

An aperture is the hole in the lens that light must pass through; it can adjust in size from large to small. Much like the human eye has an iris that changes size as the light in the room changes, your camera lens's aperture can change size to accommodate different levels of light. When the hole is large, a lot of light can pass through; when that hole is small, only a tiny amount of light can get through. The size of this hole is noted by your camera as a ratio called an f/stop. Remember: Stops work with double or half the amount of light. You may have seen numbers like f/2.8 or f/16. These are the f/stops.

F/stops are listed in an order so each each stop lets in one half the amount of light as the stop before it. They are as follows; f/1, f/1.4, f/2, f/2.8, f/4, f/5.6, f/8, f/11, f/16, f/22, f/32, f/45, f/64 etc. Most camera lenses range from about f/4 to f/22 or so. Memorizing these numbers will help you with *reciprocity* later.

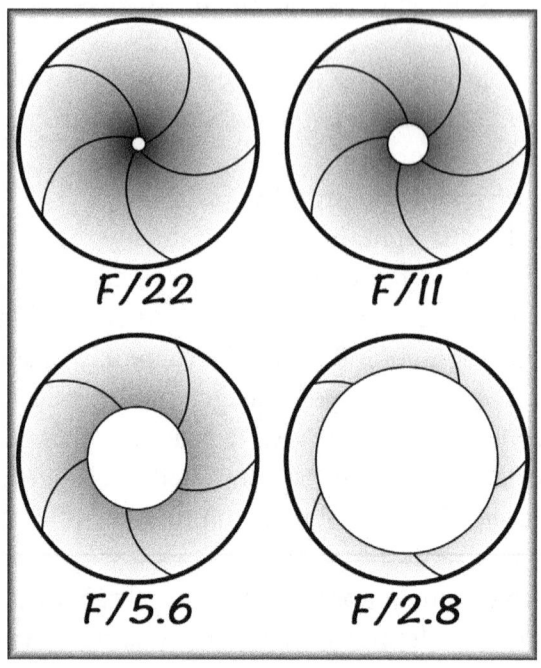

F/stop numbers may seem strange and random. They are not. That number is actually an answer to a division problem or a quotient. You will never need to know how an f/stop is calculated to take a great picture, but here is that info anyway.

We arrive at an f/stop by taking the diameter of the opening of the aperture, and dividing it by the focal length of the lens. For example if you have a 50mm lens, and the opening of the aperture is 25mm wide, you have an f/2. In this case the opening is ½ as large as the focal length. If you change that opening and make it smaller you are *stopping down* your lens, this lets less light into your camera. If that opening is just 3.125 mm on the same 50mm lens, you are at f/16 (50/3.125=16); the opening is 1/16th as large as the focal length of the lens. If the opening is again 25mm but the lens is now 100mm, that is 100mm/25mm or 1/4 or f/4. To get a 100mm lens down to f/2, the opening would have to be 50mm wide. This means a bigger and thus more expensive lens. If you have been to a pro sports game you may have noticed some photographers with gigantic lenses. While those pro lenses do have quite a zoom, there is a good chance you have a lens with a greater zoom in your camera bag. Those pro lenses are large so that they can accommodate a huge aperture. This way they can be used in low light and still collect enough light to make an image.

Understanding where these f/stop numbers come from makes it easy to understand why a small number is a big hole and a big number is a small hole. Knowing that a big hole lets in more light, you now know that you need an open aperture, or small f/stop # like f/2.8 in a dark room, and a constricted aperture, or big f/stop # like f/16 in bright sunlight. The more light you have, the smaller the aperture hole you will need.

Remember earlier we noted that the f/stop is a ratio of the aperture and lens. A stop of f/1 in a 50mm lens would have an aperture opening of 50mm. (50 / 50=1) In order to take in ½ as much light, the *area* of the aperture opening must be ½ as big (Area=πr^2). Half the area gives us a diameter of about 35.714 mm and 50/35.714 = 1.4, hence f/1.4 lets in ½ the light that f/1 does. This same rule applies to all of the f/stops.

You may have noticed that your camera has more numbers than ones we listed here. Modern cameras can set the size of the aperture to sizes between stops. This allows for greater accuracy in your exposure.

Some cameras can select apertures in half stop increments; some are more accurate and can select in third stop increments. In a full stop camera, you will go from f/8 to f/11, one full stop. In a half stop camera you will go from f/8 to f/9.5 to f/11. In a third stop camera you will go from f/8 to f/9 to f/10 to f/11. In every case it is just one stop from f/8 to f/11.

If your photos are underexposed, you can correct this by letting in more light with the aperture; if they are overexposed, you can let in less light with the aperture. Aperture is also one of two ways to control depth of field. We will cover that at the end of chapter 4.

The next way to control the amount of light your image sensor receives is with the *shutter speed.*

Shutter Speed

The shutter on a camera is a sort of sliding door. When it is open, light can pass through it to the image sensor; when it is closed no light can enter and the image sensor is in complete darkness. When you are not taking a picture, the shutter is closed. As light enters your camera, it passes through the lens containing the aperture; then it passes through the open shutter before hitting your image sensor. The amount of time your shutter is open is known as the *shutter speed,* and is normally measured in fractions of seconds. When the shutter is open longer, more light reaches the image sensor. When the shutter is open for a shorter time, less light reaches the image sensor.

Just as with aperture, shutter speed works with halves and doubles. Half the time open = half the light to the sensor; double the time open = double the light to the sensor. Unlike aperture sizes, however, these times are simple and straightforward. When your camera tells you that your shutter speed is 200, it is actually telling you that your shutter is open for 1/200th of a second. A faster shutter speed (less light) would be 400, or 1/400th of a second, or half the amount of time as 200. Most DSLR cameras range from 30 seconds to 1/4000th of a second. If your camera is set to expose for 1 second or more, the number will have a quotation mark after it. For example, 3" is three seconds.

The shutter speed *stops* that you will work with most of the time are 15, 30, 60, 100, 200, 400, 800, 1600, 2400. For the most part if you are slower than about 1/60th you will need a tripod.

Just like with aperture, controlling exposure comes down to letting in more or less light. If you are underexposed by one stop at 200, move to a shutter speed of 100; you will let in double the light, and your exposure will be correct. If you are overexposed by one stop at 200, move to 400 you will let in half the amount of light, and your exposure will be correct.

Just as with aperture, shutter speed also has ½ & ⅓ stops. A change from 100 to 200 is a change of one full stop; 100 to 125 is ⅓ of a stop; 125 to 160 is ⅓ of a stop and so on; 100 to 150 is ½ of a stop and so on. Most of the time you can choose to have your camera to work with full stops, half stops, or third stops.

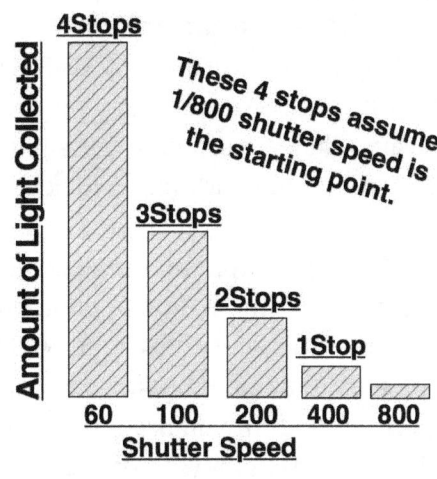

Shutter speed affects more than just exposure. If you have your shutter open for a long time like 1/15th, or 15, you will be able to gather light as a subject is moving. This will create a blurry image. If you have your shutter open for a short time, your image will freeze the movement of your subject and your image will be more crisp. If you are photographing a hummingbird in flight, the wings of that bird will almost disappear completely at 1/60th of a second. To *pause* the wings of that bird and photograph them as a crisp object, you will have to have a fast shutter speed like 1/4000th of a second or so. Likewise, if you are taking a photo of a waterfall at a slow shutter speed, the water will have a nice blur to it. This will give your photograph the feeling of motion. If you use a fast shutter speed, you will completely stop the motion of the falls, and you will capture an image that is crisp and appears to be motionless.

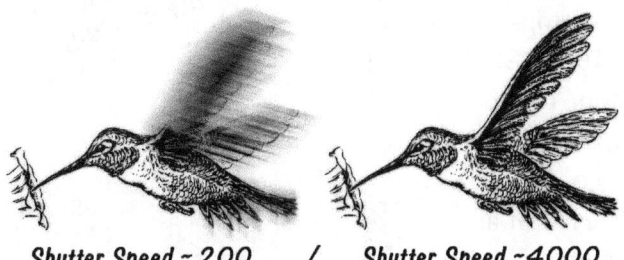

Shutter Speed ~ 200 / Shutter Speed ~4000

Original image courtesy of the U.S. Library of Congress public domain clipart gallery, edited for this book by Jason Youn.

ISO - The camera's sensitivity to light

There is no reason to be scared of the ISO setting on your camera. I have known many people who just leave this on auto, because they are afraid to mess things up. While using the wrong ISO can make your images look grainy, selecting the proper ISO will make choosing the f/stop and shutter speed much easier.

ISO is an acronym that stands for International Standards Organization. In relation to photography, this number indicates your camera's sensitivity to light. This sensitivity is adjustable. You may remember buying camera film with different *speeds.* The speed of the film you used to buy is noted buy the ISO number. The ISO setting on your digital camera is just like that. This is one of the best parts of shooting digital. In a world of film, changing ISO meant you had to remove the film from your camera and replace it with different film. Or you could carry several camera bodies, one with each film you want to use. With digital, you can move from one ISO to another and back again with ease.

ISO is expressed with a number. A low ISO number like 100 is not as light sensitive and requires more light to make an image, while a high number like 1600 is very sensitive to light and will require less light to create a well exposed image.

As with aperture and shutter speed, ISO once again works in halves and doubles. The normal *stops* are 100, 200, 400, 800, 1600, and so on.

Just as with aperture & shutter speed, your cameras ISO settings may have ½ & ⅓ stops available. 100 to 200 is one full stop; 100 to 125 is ⅓ of a stop; 125 to 160 is ⅓ of a stop; 100 to 150 is ½ of a stop, and so on.

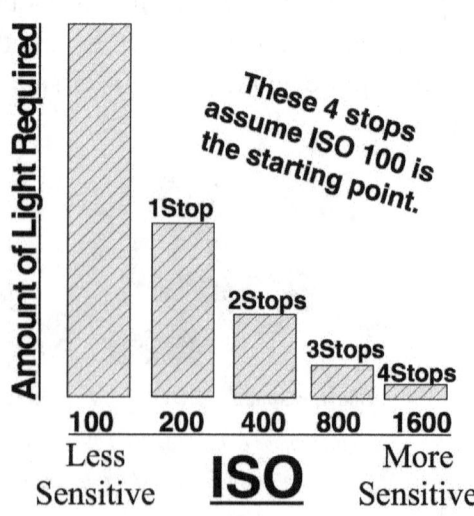

As with everything in photography, ISO comes with a trade off. You will normally get less digital noise like grain and color noise at lower ISOs. At high ISOs your camera will require less light to operate, but you will introduce more noise into the photograph.

You don't need to be afraid to shoot at high ISO settings. Sometimes, sacrificing a little image quality to get the shot you want is worth it. I routinely print images taken at 1600+ ISO. As technology gets better, that ability to shoot a fine quality image at a high ISO will continue to get better. The cameras that are just on the horizon can shoot at ISO 128,000 and look good at 24,000.

Just remember to change your ISO back when you go out into the sunlight. Otherwise, your camera will be forced to shoot at 8000 shutter speed with and aperture of f/22 just to keep the exposure correct and your images will have much more grain than necessary.

Reciprocity

Reciprocity is the relationship between shutter speed, aperture, and ISO. The idea behind reciprocity is simple. Your camera needs just the right amount of light to create a photograph. If you allow more light in your camera one way, you must remove it in another way. You can add and remove light 4 ways: *ambient light* - add or remove light from your actual setting; *aperture* - make the hole in your lens bigger or smaller; *shutter speed* - increase or decrease the amount of time the shutter is open; *ISO* - change how sensitive your image sensor is to light.

Here is an example. If proper exposure is f/8 at 1/250th at ISO 200, and you decide you want your aperture to be at f/4, you are now letting in 2 stops more light, or double and then double again, or 4 times the amount of light, because the aperture is 2 stops larger. Your image is now 2 stops overexposed. To bring the image back to proper exposure, you must either adjust the shutter speed, or the ISO, or both. If you adjust the shutter speed you need to make it 2 stops faster, that new speed would be 1/1000th (noted on your camera as 1000). If on the other hand you adjust the ISO, you will need to make your camera two stops less light sensitive, so your new ISO would be 50. This concept is called *reciprocity*. The following chart shows ISO, shutter, & aperture.

It is set up so that, if you have decided on your three settings and you want to change just one setting, you can do it with ease. Here's how it works. If you move any one setting to the right or to the left, you must move another setting in the opposite direction. In the example shown, f/8 is changed to f/4. This is a move of two stops. To compensate, the shutter speed is moved two stops in the opposite direction, from 250 to 1000. If you can keep this concept in mind, choosing the right setting for proper exposure will be simple.

Reciprocity

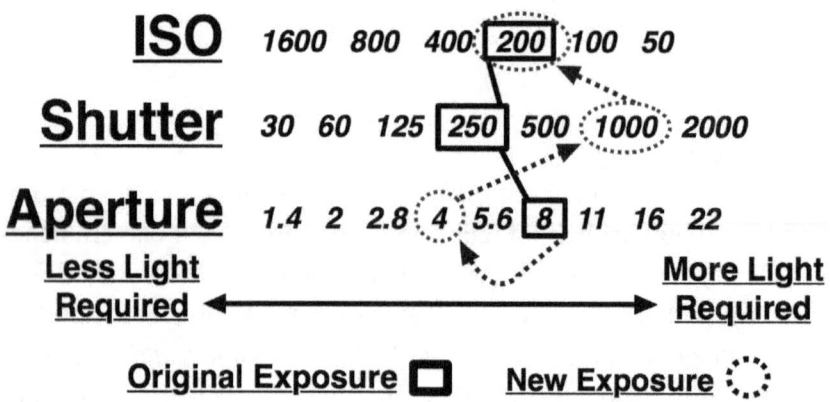

ISO 1600 800 400 200 100 50

Shutter 30 60 125 250 500 1000 2000

Aperture 1.4 2 2.8 4 5.6 8 11 16 22

Less Light Required ← → **More Light Required**

Original Exposure ▢   **New Exposure** ⫶⫶

Color Temperature

Color temperature is a scientific way of notating how warm or cool light appears to be. If you have ever looked at a photo and thought, wow that looks too orange, or too blue, congratulations, you are well on your way to getting proper color balance.

Photographs can look too orange or too blue because the lights that we encounter in our day-to-day lives have a hue to them. There is pure white light, but we almost never encounter it. Every light bulb has a color; the sun has a color; a candle flame has a color. We measure that color in Degrees Kelvin, noted simply as K.

Color temperature is not a reference to the actual thermal energy of light. Rather it is a reference to a simple science experiment. In the late 1800s, William Thompson or Lord Kelvin applied heat to a block of pure carbon. Somewhere around 1000 degrees Kelvin (a scientific way to measure heat, like Fahrenheit or centigrade), the block began to glow a dull reddish orange. As the block was heated more, the color shifted to orange, then yellow, then white, then finally around 10,000 degrees Kelvin, blue.

For color temperature, we say Kelvin, but we are not talking about heat; we are referring to the color produced by carbon at that given thermal temperature. We note that color as K. If we are talking about heat we say degrees Kelvin.

A normal incandescent light bulb is about 2800 K. The light from your camera's flash is 6000 K. It just so happens that normal sunlight is around 5500 K but that can change depending on the time of year, part of the world, altitude, time of day, cloud cover, pollution levels, and my daughter's mood. In order to correct for this difference in color, your camera can balance the light. This is the *white balance.*

When a white balance is set to a given color temperature, say for instance the flash setting (6000 K), you are telling your camera that the color of light from a flash (6000 K) is pure white. Any light that is lower than 6000 K will look orange; any light that is above 6000 K will look blue. The intensity of that color will increase as its distance from the white point increases. If you set your camera's white balance to the incandescent light bulb setting, you are telling your camera that white light is about 2800 K. Anything below that is orange and above that is blue.

Our eyes and brain have this feature built in. Without thinking, we automatically adjust the information that our eyes collect, and we color balance the world around us to make white look white. Try this: If you look at a white slip of paper in your living room at night by candle light, you will actually be seeing a paper that is reflecting orange light; in that sense, you are looking at an orange paper. Because our brain tells us that the paper is white, we still see it as white. Cameras cannot do this. We must white balance for them.

There are four ways of white balancing in your camera. First, you can simply leave your camera on the auto white balance mode. Sometimes this is the best way to go. It's easy and the camera generally does a fairly good job. The downside, however, is that each and every photograph has its own unique white balance setting. This can make editing more difficult. If you have 500 photographs and each one has the same white balance issues, you can batch edit them and fix all of them at one time. If all of them are just a little different, than you will have to fix each one individually. For all its downsides however, auto white balance is fast and convenient.

The next thing you can do is select one of the camera's built-in white balance settings. Most cameras have a setting for sun, shade, overcast, tungsten lightbulb, fluorescent lightbulb, and flash. Your camera's manual will have more info on how this works for your individual camera. The nice thing about these settings is that it's easy to use and constant from one shot to the next. It is not perfectly accurate, but it's really close.

Next you can select the exact temperature K in your camera's menu. This will give you a lot of creative control over what you are photographing. If you are too warm, you just drop down a few K; if you are too cool, you just come up a few K. This is a very accurate way to work. The downside is that this can take some real getting used to, but depending on your shooting style, it can be worth the extra time.

The last way to adjust for the color of light is a custom white balance. This is done by taking a test shot of a white card or anything that is white, and then telling your camera that "this is white." Your camera will then use that as the white point. This is the most accurate way to work, but this takes the most time to set up, and most of the time it is not the way to go. If you are doing scientific work, or product photography, where color is absolutely essential, you may want to consider using this custom white balance setting.

Once you have captured your photo, you can usually work on the white balance more when you edit the images on your computer. It is, however, important to get at least a fairly good white balance in the camera. If this sounds hard, don't worry; this will be easy with just a little practice.

Next time you are at a large hardware store, stop by the lighting department. You will probably see a setup with several different kinds of light bulbs shining on a fabric or color card. These are set up to show off the different color temperatures available. Some will be CFL, some LED, and some will be incandescent. For my money, the best light for home use comes from quartz halogen bulbs.

Lenses

Our eyes and brain have the ability to focus on one object in the center of our vision or take in an entire world and see what is going on across a panorama of vision. Camera lenses are not as versatile, however. To do what our eyes do, the camera needs several lenses. Thankfully, with the correct lens, the camera can do more than just our eyes alone.

The lens is the round glass on the front of your camera that light passes through on its way to the image sensor; it focuses and controls the light that your camera takes in.

SLR cameras have several lenses to choose from, and they are interchangeable. Some zoom, some don't. Some will act like a telescope and take you way in, some will capture the entire room, and some will focus down on a single grain of rice. Some distort the world and some do not.

Every camera has a lens that will more closely match the world as the human eye sees it. It won't enlarge the world, make it smaller, or distort it. It won't be zoomed in or out; it will just cause the photo to look much as the world looks in real life. This type of lens is called a *normal* lens.

For all cameras the hypotenuse of the sensor is what gives us the size of its normal lens. A full frame 35mm camera has a sensor size of 36x24mm. The hypotenuse of that rectangle is about 43mm long, so a 43mm lens would be perfect. The next closest thing commonly on the market is a 50mm prime, so a 50mm lens is considered to be the normal lens for a 35mm full frame camera. If you shoot a DSLR with a crop sensor like the APS-C, then the normal lens is about 35mm. If you use a micro four thirds sensor camera, your normal lens is only about 25mm.

In every case the field of view is about 40 degrees horizontally for a normal lens. In other words, an image from a 35mm camera with a 50 mm lens is about the same as an image from an APS-C camera with a 35mm lens, and that is about the same as an image from a four thirds camera with a 25mm lens. They all take in 40 degrees of the surrounding environment when measured horizontally or longways. If a lens takes in more than about 40 degrees, it is a wide angle lens; if it takes in less than about 40 degrees, it is a telephoto. Commonly, photographers refer to wide angle lenses as *short lenses* and telephoto lenses as *long lenses*.

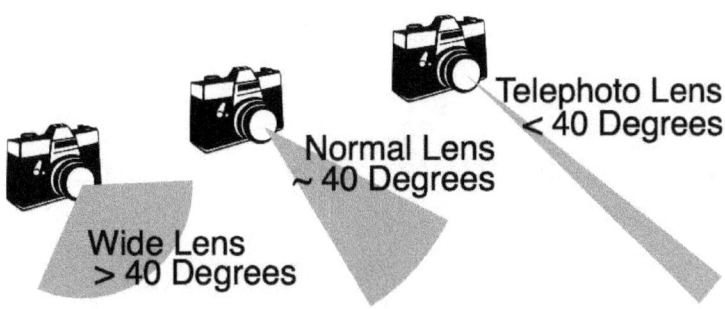

Normal lenses, wide angle lenses, and telephoto lenses all have different characteristics and will produce different images.

Three Lens Types & Attributes

Wide Angle Lenses

- A larger area than normal fits into your camera frame. This is handy when you cannot move your camera back any farther, like for an indoor group shot.

- Objects in your camera will look smaller at the same focal distance when compared to a normal lens.

- It exaggerates depth or distance as it recedes from the camera. For instance an object will look further away from its background than it really is.

Wide Angle Lenses Continued...

- Camera shake is less noticeable; thus, you can hand-hold your camera at a slower shutter speed.

- Features of your subject become more spread out and distorted, especially near the edge of the frame. A portrait may have a large nose and smaller ears for example.

- Extreme wide angle lenses cause straight lines to appear to bend and distort as they cross through the frame.

Normal Lenses

- Normal lenses will show the world in a manner that is similar to how our eye sees it.

- 40 degrees horizontally of your surroundings will fit into your frame.

- Depth and perspective will look normal.

- Features of your subject appear much as they do in real life.

Telephoto Lens

- A smaller than normal area fits into your camera's frame. Much like a set of binoculars, this lens is good for subjects that are far away when you do not have the ability to move closer, like at a sports game or in wildlife photography.

- Objects in your camera if photographed from the same distance will appear to be larger when compared to a normal lens.

- It compresses depth or distance as it recedes from the camera. For instance, an object will look closer to its background.

- Camera shake is more noticeable; thus you must have a faster shutter speed to hand hold a telephoto lens.

- Features of your subject become flat, i.e. the distance from front to back of your subject appears to lessen.

Zoom & Prime Lenses

Your camera probably came with a kit lens that has the ability to zoom. There is another kind of lens out there however. A lens that doesn't zoom in or out is known as a fixed focal length or *prime lens*. Because prime lenses do not have to change their internal configuration to zoom in or out, they have fewer pieces of glass inside of them. As a result, the image quality of a given lens is generally higher with a `prime lens. Having less glass also means that a prime lens is a lot lighter and easier to carry around. I keep a 50mm f/1.4 on had at all times. It is not heavy, relatively cheap, packs well, is great in low light, and has a nice small depth of field when the aperture is wide. The down side to a prime lens is that, if you want to change focal lengths, you must change lenses. Zoom lenses do not have this problem; a zoom lens can change its focal length with one simple motion.

Most lenses sold today are zoom lenses. Their ability to go from wide to normal to telephoto makes them the perfect choice for many photographers. If you want a wider frame, zoom out; if you want a tighter frame, zoom in. These lenses do weigh more, take up more space, and generally cost more money to get the same quality of image. The ability to quickly select your desired focal length and then quickly change it again usually makes the added weight, cost, and loss of quality worth dealing with.

Focus

Just like with our eyes, an image captured with a camera can be in focus or out of focus. When something is in focus, it appears sharp, clear, and crisp. When it's out of focus, it appears soft, blurry and fuzzy. We don't consciously focus our eyes because our brain and eyes actually manipulate the shape of a lens in our eye automatically. Like our eyes, cameras also have lenses. Our camera, however, cannot change the shape of its lens to focus. Rather, it must move the focusing lens, or *element* back and forth to achieve optimal focus.

Before being able to properly focus your camera, your diopter should be properly adjusted. This device is in the reticle or viewfinder of your camera. The diopter allows the viewfinder to be adjusted for your individual eye. Notice the small adjustment wheel near the eyecup of your viewfinder? This will move a lens back and forth in your eyepiece so that an in focus image in your camera will look in focus to your eye. To make this adjustment on a DSLR or SLR, carefully remove the lens from your camera. Look through your eyepiece and aim your camera at a blank wall. Now adjust the wheel until the lines and or boxes in your reticle come into optimal focus. Your reticle should looks something like this. The small boxes are the autofocus points. If you have vertical or horizontal lines, they are there to help you compose your image. Once your diopter is adjusted and the boxes are in focus, carefully replace your cameras 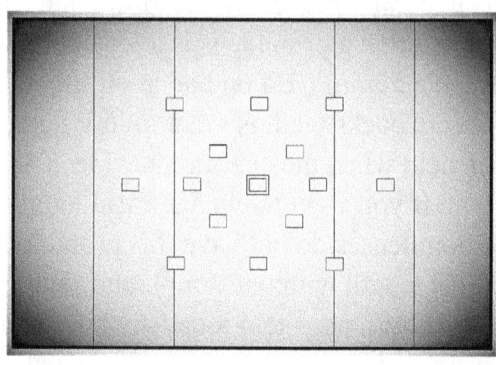 lens. Your camera is now adjusted for your eye.

There are two basic types of focusing, auto focus and manual focus. Most modern cameras do a fine job of auto focusing. If you want to leave your camera on full auto focus, the computer inside your camera will decide for itself where to place its focal points. Often this is a good way to go; it is simple and can work well, but you lose a bit of control with this method. If you want to use auto focus, but you still want to have control over which part of the image is in focus, you can use selectable auto focus points and auto focus lock.

Auto focus points

Auto focus points are the dots inside your cameras reticle that the auto focus sensor uses to focus your image. Your camera has many of them and in full auto mode your camera automatically selects the points that it thinks are best and uses those to focus. You can probably see these points within your camera's eyepiece. If you want more control, however, you can tell the camera what focus point to use. If you select an AF point the camera will always use that point to select its auto focus. But what do you do if that point you have selected is not the point of the photograph that you want to have in focus? This is where *Auto Focus / Exposure Lock* comes in handy.

Auto Focus Lock,

Auto focus lock, or AE/AF lock tells your camera to focus, select its exposure, and then hold those settings. Once it is engaged your camera will not refocus. AF lock is used by pressing your shutter release button halfway down. (You may have to turn on your AE/AF lock in your cameras settings). Look through the view finder, find the spot that you want to have in focus and frame your camera so that your selected auto focus point is over that spot. Press the shutter release button half way down. Re-frame your image so that the composition is the way that you want it to be. Notice your camera will not re-focus. Now press the shutter release button the rest of the way down. Your camera will take a photograph.

Manual Focus

Being able to focus your camera on your own, without the AF assistance, is an important tool to have at your disposal. Not only does it give you complete control over your focus, sometimes it's your only option. You may have noticed that your camera has a hard or even impossible time focusing in low light. When this happens manual focus is your best option. First place your camera in manual focus mode. Consult your cameras owner's manual on how this is done. Some lenses now have a manual focus scale on them. If this is the case, you can just set the lens to the correct distance and you are focused. If you can't focus that way, simply look through your camera's eyepiece and twist the focus ring on the lens back and forth until the image looks its sharpest. Once your image is focused, take your photograph. If you have done all this correctly, your image will be in focus. If you are in a tough situation and focus is hard to achieve, try using a larger depth of field. If your depth of field is large enough, your focus can be way off and your image will still look to be in focus.

Depth of Field

The subject that your camera focuses on may not be the only thing in focus. Depth of field is the space in front of your camera where the image looks to be in focus. It is not just what you focus on. For example you may focus on something that is 15 feet away, but your depth-of-field may very well be from 10 feet to 25 feet. So if your subject is between 10 feet and 25 feet from your camera, it will be in focus.

As with most things in photography, there are many ways to control your depth of field. You can control it with the *focal length* of your lens, the *aperture size*, and your subject's *distance from the camera*.

Assuming the camera and subject do not change location, the depth of field decreases as the focal length of the lens increases. So a longer lens, like a telephoto, creates a smaller depth of field, and a shorter lens, like a normal or wide angle lens, creates a larger depth of field. So a wide angle lens has a larger depth of field than a telephoto lens at the same aperture and focal distance. The simplest and most common way to control your depth of field, however, is with your aperture.

You already know that your aperture is used to control exposure, but there is another function. Depth of field increases as the size of the aperture decreases. That is to say your depth of field is much larger at f/22 than it is at f/2.8. Aperture is the primary way to control your depth of field. If you want to make a portrait, where the background is blurred out, shoot with a wide open aperture (f/2.8, for example). If you are shooting action sports or wildlife photography and your subject is moving around rapidly, perfect focus may be difficult, so shoot at a smaller aperture like f/11 or f/16. Most landscape photographers shoot their work on a tripod with a very stopped down aperture, such as f/22 or higher. You can force your camera to use the aperture you want by either shooting in full manual mode or by selecting aperture priority.

The last thing that affects depth of field is the distance from the subject to the camera. A close subject will yield a smaller depth of field and a distant subject will create a larger depth of field.

Apart from being able to control the size of your depth of field, it is important to know the *2/3rd Rule*. The depth of field is always situated in a way where 1/3 of what is in focus is in front of your focal point and 2/3 are behind the focal point. For example, if your depth of field is 15 feet long, then the 5 feet in front of your focal point will be in focus, and 10 behind your focal point will be in focus.

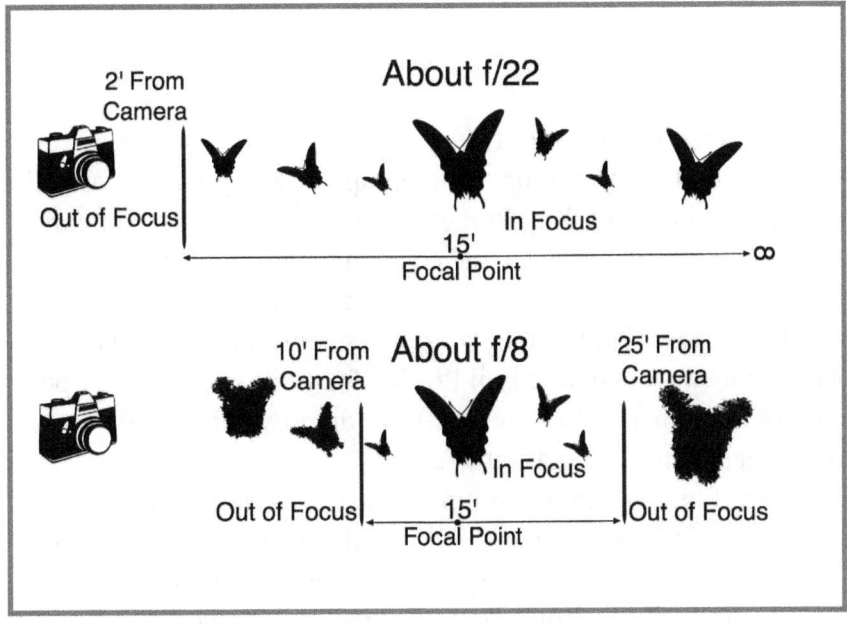

Composition & Other

Rules of Art

Painting With Light

The first time I went on a photographic expedition, it was still the good old days of film. Proper camera work was more important because you couldn't guess and check like you can with a digital SLR camera. If you made a mistake or miscalculation, you wouldn't know about it until your prints came back from the lab. Most of us were shooting Fuji Pro-V 35mm film at about $11 per roll (plus another $6 to develop it); we didn't want to waste shots on miscalculated camera settings.

One of the girls in our group had a strong background in painting and that was about it. She would ask questions like what is an f/stop, or what do you mean wide angle lens? We all thought her photos would turn out poorly done and overexposed or out of focus. The last night of the trip was show and tell night. We all got together and showed off our past work and images from the trip. Everyone's was good; some were great. For the group I was sub-par, but I was young and didn't have much time behind the lens. Soon it was that poor confused painter's turn. You could tell most of us in the room thought her images would be a waste of time. We were wrong. Her photos were stunning. Her composition, weight and balance, use of color, line, and shape were all without match for the room. The girl who knew nothing about cameras (read: nothing about chapters 2, 3, & 4) took us all to school. All she did was turn her camera to landscape mode for landscape and portrait mode for people. For the landscape shots she used a tripod. She used her carefully honed knowledge of composition and art and the camera did the rest.

I tell you this story not to convince you to forget about chapters 2 through 4; rather, I tell it to encourage you. It's good to know your camera inside and out. It's better if you can calculate reciprocity quickly and on the spot. But don't worry if you forget a thing or two about your camera. If you keep in mind the simple principles of art, you will do fine. If a picture is worth a thousand words, composition is the language. A well composed photograph is like a well written book. The girl with no clue how to use her camera had a background in painting; she knew how to compose an image. While the rest of us were taking photographs and snapshots, she was painting with light.

Use a Tripod

I have been asked time and again for advice on what kind of camera gear to buy. Most of the time the answer is a good tripod and an off-camera shutter release button. For this you will need to go to a camera store, not Best Buy. The tripod should be sturdy and well made. Get ready to spend at least $100 on the tripod, minimum.

Hand holding a camera while you take a picture only works if your shutter is fast enough to keep the image from looking blurry. If the shutter is open for too long and your camera is not on a tripod, your image will blur. One simple way to know if your shutter speed requires you to use a tripod is the *1/focal length rule.*

To hand hold a 50mm lens, your shutter speed should be 1/50th of a second or faster on full frame camera and 1.5x that speed (1/75th) on a crop sensor SLR. If the shutter speed is too slow, you will introduce camera shake and your image will have a shaky blurry quality. With a good tripod, you can keep that shutter open for as long as you want. If your subjects are moving too quickly, they may be blurry, but the camera shake will be eliminated.

Most cameras will let you set the shutter speed to stay open for as much as 30 seconds, but with an off-camera shutter release button with either a built-in timer or button lock mode, you can keep that shutter open for as long as you like. There are two more benefits to the off-camera button. One, even on a tripod, your hand can introduce camera shake when you touch the camera to take the picture. Two, sometimes it can be uncomfortable to reach over and press the on-camera button to take a new photo. Your tripod may be high up or at a weird angle. The off-camera button will let you keep your hands where you like.

The next benefit of a tripod is that it forces you to <u>take your time and compose your shot with care</u>. Rather than running and gunning like a seasoned press photographer, tripod users have to think carefully about what they are doing. Good composition is a cornerstone of good photography, or any art for that matter. You can literally set your camera to full auto mode and if your composition is good enough, your photo will turn out great.

The Rule of Thirds

Perhaps the most widely talked about and best known artistic principal is the *Rule of Thirds*.

These days it's a common rule that all artist learn, but it was only recently that the Rule of Thirds was given a name. The first known reference comes from Sir Joshua Reynolds in his book *Remarks on Rural Scenery*, (1797). Discussing dominant and subordinate areas of light and dark in a painting, he noted that one should be larger than the other. Reynolds named this principle the Rule of Thirds, and it has since become a staple of design theory.

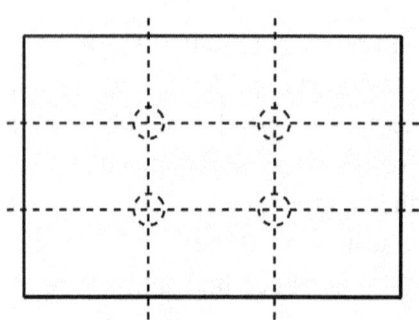

The idea is simple; divide a rectangular image vertically into thirds, and horizontally into thirds. The dividing lines are where interesting subjects should be placed within the image. The four points where the lines meet should normally be the focal points of your image. Think of the rule of thirds as a good starting point for composing your image.

The next few images show the same scene, The left, for the most part, does not use the Rule of Thirds. The right image, for the most part, does use the Rule of Thirds. In the first image the tree is in the middle of the frame left to right, and the horizon is in the middle top to bottom. Notice how the composition is improved by moving the tree to the left third line, and placing the horizon on the bottom third line.

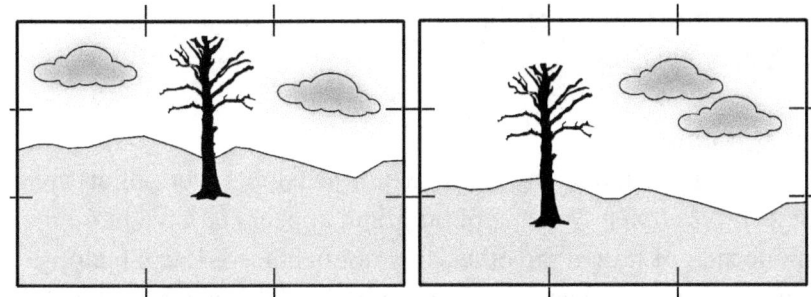

Below a football player reaches to catch a ball. The left image is not composed well. In the right image, the player's face is on the right third line and the football is at the intersection of the left and top line. The framing has less unused, or negative, space.

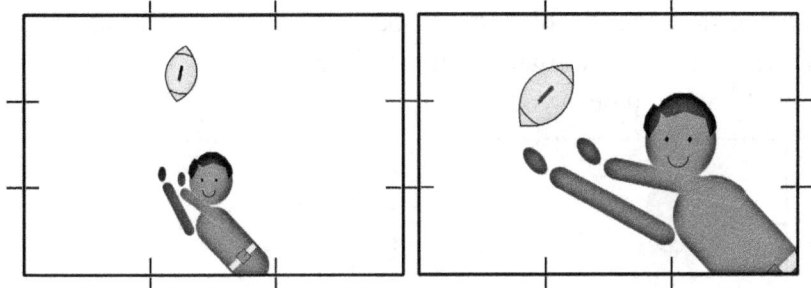

In this last example, the left image shows a face of a man just placed in the center of the frame. In the right image, his eyes are on the third line, and his shoulders are on the third line. There is also less unused space above his head.

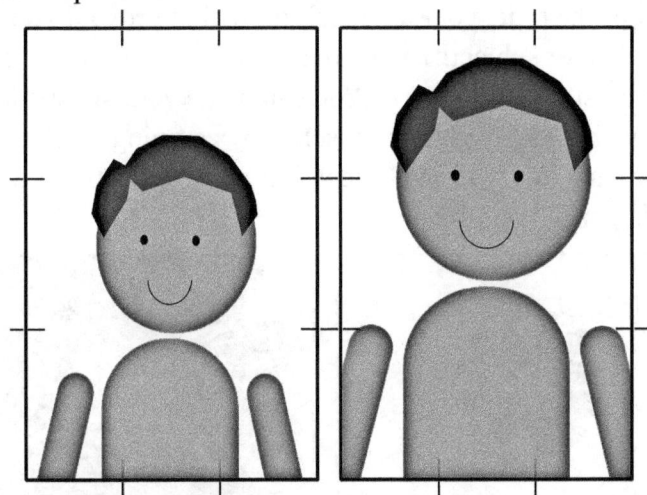

Many times the composition of an image can have major improvements with just small camera movements. By using the Rule of Thirds, we were able to improve each of these images with just minor changes.

Balance

Photographs, like any other two dimensional work of art are subject to *balance.* When a photograph appears to have more mass on one side of it than the other, it is not balanced. It can be top heavy, left or right heavy, or bottom heavy. This can have the effect of giving the viewer an uneasy feeling. To fix this, you can place another object on the other side of the frame. This will help to balance out your composition.

Because negative space, or empty space, plays a role in composition, the two objects do not have to be the same size or shape; rather, it is normally better if they are not the same size, though they can be if you like.

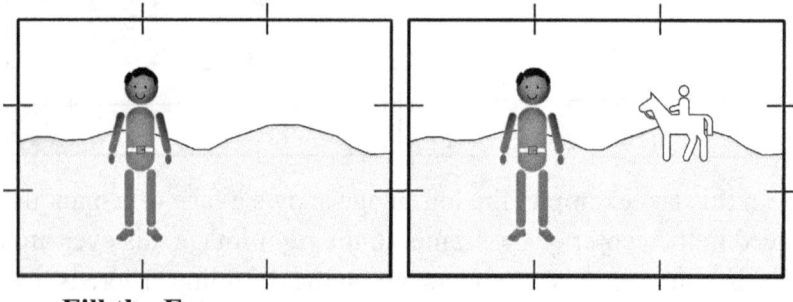

Fill the Frame

Most of the time, your composition will improve if you fill the frame with your subject. There are of course times when this is not true, but most of the time it is. You can make your subject larger in your frame by simply getting closer or by zooming in. Each action will have a slightly different effect, but both will make your subject larger in your image.

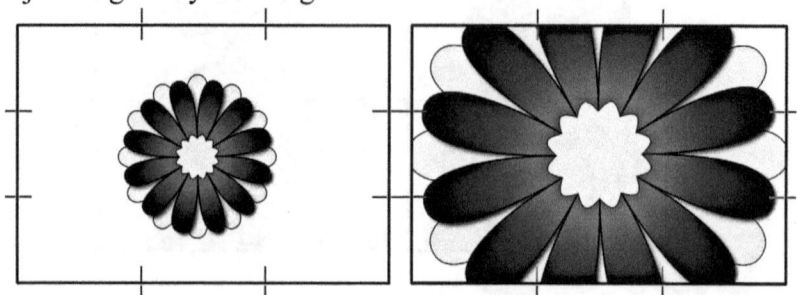

Color & Brightness

When working with color or black and white, keep in mind that the brighter or bolder color will attract attention. If you have a bright spot in your photograph, or a bold color in your image, the viewer will focus on it, even if it's not an intended part of the composition. If you have a bright spot, you can try to make that a focal point, or cut it out of the scene all together to avoid distracting your audience. If it's in the frame, people will notice it. Bright colors also appear to have more mass or weight in a photograph than muted ones. If you have two equally sized shapes, one bright and the other dim, the brighter portion will overpower the dimmer section of your work. If you can't get rid of the offending object, incorporate it. Perhaps you can balance it with another object.

In the 1950's, an artist named Mark Rothko created paintings of colored rectangles. Though many of his works are simple, they still manage to appeal to a wide audience in a positive way. My favorite is just two rectangles. The larger shape is blue and the smaller one is the complement of blue, which is orange. The blue takes up the top two thirds of the frame and the smaller orange rectangle is just the bottom one third. This simple work of art is an excellent example of how color and brightness can be used to balance an image. Just as size and shape can create balance, complementary colors can be used to balance each other out. In Rothko's painting, the brighter warmer color, orange, is more dominant. If the colors were given equal position, the orange would overpower the blue. Rothko made the blue twice the size of the orange, and in doing so, achieved balance.

Frame Within a Frame

A frame within a frame is just about as simple as it sounds. Imagine an apple pie cooling in a farmhouse window on a summer day. Did you imagine the window frame and curtains around the pie? Or did you just imagine the windowsill without anything else? The framing of window curtains help to make the image more interesting, it can provide balance, it narrows down the viewer's selection and provides a more intimate setting for the pie to cool.

This concept of frame within a frame can be achieved with architecture, trees, people, clouds, lighting, or just about anything. Pay attention for it when you watch a movie; guaranteed, you will see it being used. Below a man is standing in a field waving. In the left picture he is alone; in the right, a tree creates a frame within a frame effect. Which do you think has a stronger composition?

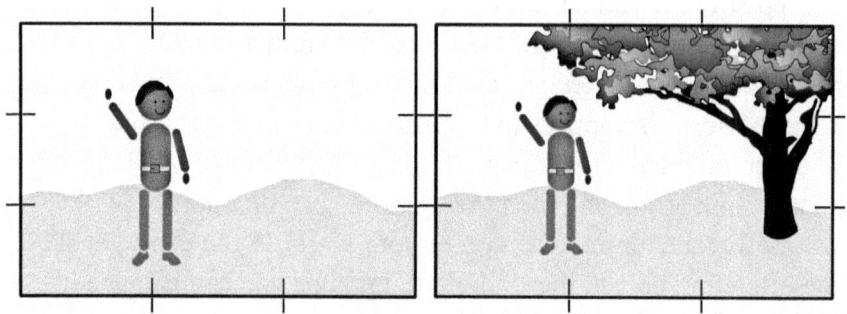

Leading Lines

Our eyes naturally want to follow lines and arrows; we're just set up that way. If you see a set of power lines receding into the distance, your eyes will follow them. If there is an arrow on a sign, your brain will tend to look for something that the arrow is pointing to. These lines lead you to another object or part of a composition.

Leading lines have been used in art for hundreds of years. The Renaissance painters and sculptors were famous for using them in everything from architecture and paintings to statues and furniture. One of my favorite examples is Fra Angelico's "The Annunciation." The lines in this work are so bold that they simply cannot be overlooked.

Often leading lines are more subtle, but they will still draw the viewer's eye to a given point. Perhaps they will lead the viewer around the image in a loop over and over again. If they are not used correctly they can confuse the viewer or lead their eye out of the frame altogether. Understanding how to use leading lines will make your images stronger, and they will help your viewers understand what your photograph is all about.

Below, the focal point is the setting sun, but the sun is a muted color, so it's less likely to attract attention with its own weight, and it's not at one of the four intersection points of the rule of thirds, so it's not going to be quickly noticed. It is on the top horizontal third line, and thats good, but the leading lines are what move the viewer's eyes to the focal point. The road leads the viewers right to the sun. All of the trees make nice little arrows that point to the sky; once in the sky the crepuscular rays of the sunlight also form arrows that lead and point to the sun. Once the viewer is at the sun, the spikes coming from the sun then encourage to viewer to move away from the middle and back into the surrounding landscape where the aforementioned leading lines bring the viewer back to the center again. The mountains that hug the sun and the trees that line the road create a nice frame within a frame.

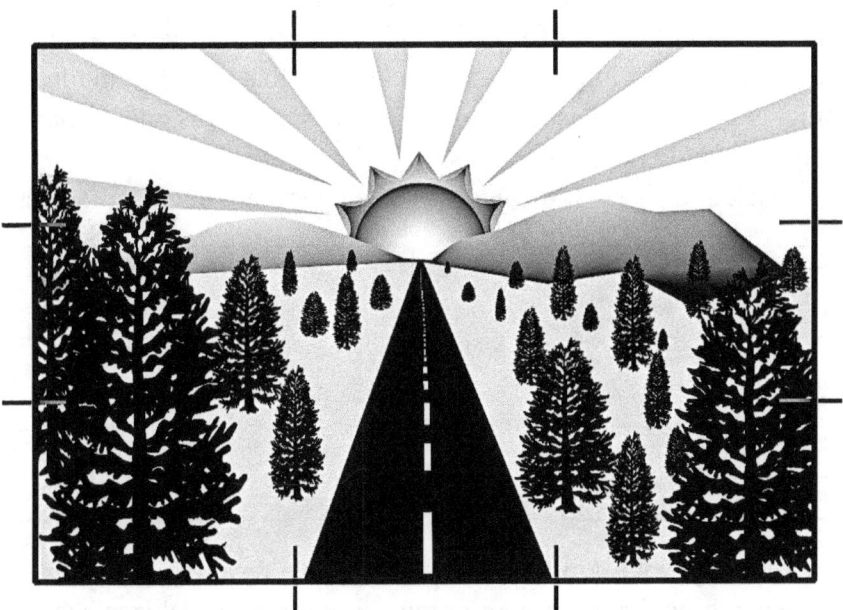

Leading Looks

Just like leading lines, leading looks can cause your viewer's eyes to move about the image. We are all trained to tune in to people's faces. Like an arrow, they point in the direction that they face. If the image is not balanced to account for leading looks, it will lead the viewer's eye right out of the image.

For the most part it is good to place the subject so that their eyes point inward toward the middle of the frame, not off of the nearest edge of the work. Having a subject placed so that they are looking to the close edge of the frame rather than the far can create a feeing that your subject is trapped, or boxed in, and it will cause an uneasy and disturbing feeling. Most of the time this is bad, but perhaps that feeling of being trapped is what you want. Alfred Hitchcock was famous for giving his audiences a nerve-racking and unsettling feeling. Framing a subject so that their leading looks quickly urged the viewer off of the movie screen was one of many ways he would accomplish this.

Look at the next few images. The subjects are identical in each.

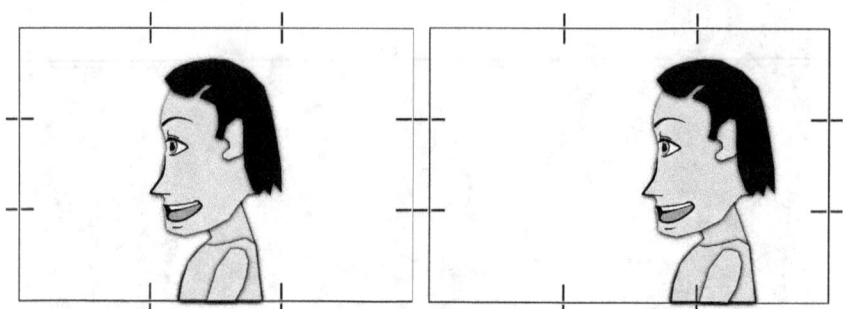

Leading looks don't have to come from a face; they can come from anything that moves, or points, or anthropomorphizes itself. In the images of the truck and the skier, the left images have the leading look pointed out of the frame, The right images have the leading looks pointed into the frame.

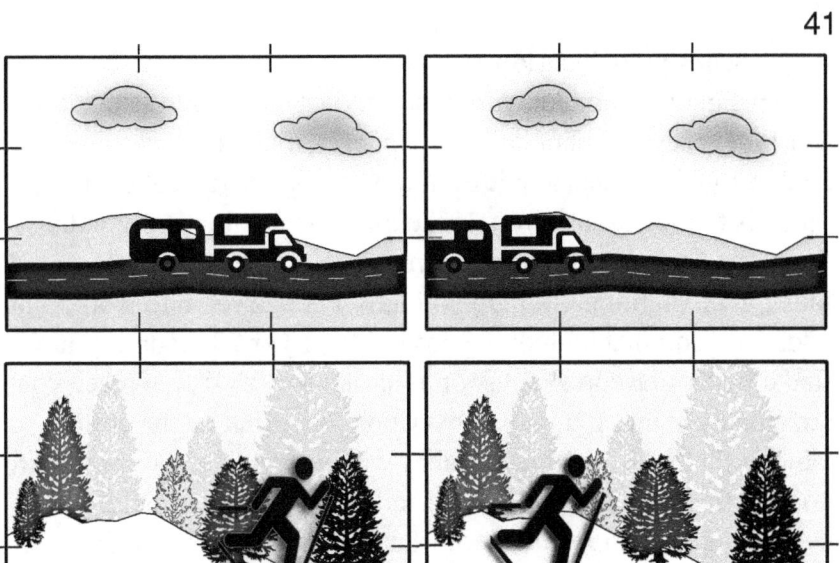

Backgrounds

Backgrounds can be boring or interesting, plain or complex, but a background should never become the foreground. How many times have you gotten your photos back, or seen them posted on Facebook, and there's a tree or flagpole growing right out of the top of someone's head? Or perhaps there is a bright object that just steals your attention away from the intended subject. Or perhaps there is something with words on it, like an exit sign, or a billboard. Your viewers will find meaning in those words. That ugly, unfortunate background becomes part of the composition whether you like it or not.

The trick with backgrounds is to keep them in the background. In the case where a tree or flagpole is growing out of your subject's head, just move a bit. Find a slightly different angle. If the background is too busy, try finding a new background, or put that background out of focus. That nice blur can make an otherwise distracting backdrop look good. Underexposing or overexposing your background can be another great way to make it less noticeable. Also, don't be afraid to ask your subjects to move a few feet to either side. Trust me; they won't mind moving.

Scout your location

This may sound like work that you just don't need to be doing. But for every good shot, at least some scouting is in order. It could be that a group wants a quick photograph at a party. Take a few seconds to look around you. Is the place where they are standing really the best place to make an image? How does the background look? Is the lighting OK? Do you have enough room to work? The odds are good that by looking around for 10 or 20 seconds you will find a better place to shoot -- or at least a way to fix the place you are already using. It's easy to overlook that drink on the coffee table or that fake plant that clashes with everything. Our brains are good at finding the information needed and then overlooking everything else. In real life, we filter out the drink, or we don't notice the plant; however, a camera will record all the stuff that you just don't want to see.

I often shoot houses for real-estate. These houses have nothing in them, just walls, ceiling fans, carpets, and electrical outlets. I can tell you from experience that when you walk into an empty house, unless you're an electrician, you probably don't notice all of the outlets. When looking at a photo of the same room, however, all of a sudden, the outlets are everywhere. They are annoying little white dots that pollute the natural beauty of the room. Our brains remove them, but the camera records them, and they are obvious in a print. That plastic cup or magazine left on a table will do the exact same thing. Go on and move it out of your frame; you will be glad you did.

For a more in-depth shoot, real scouting is required. When I shoot a wedding, or any other major shoot, I scout it out the day before. I talk to the people who work there. I walk around. I look high and low for that shot, and I make a mental note of the ugly spaces or bad angles. Let's say it's time for the bouquet toss; if the location is not familiar, how will you know where to stand? How will you know where to place your lights?

The best way to get a sunset landscape shot is to be set up before the sun goes down. If you are shooting landscape, find your locations long before the lighting is the way you want it to be. Scouting your location is a great way to make your shots better.

Of course with digital photography it's reasonable to tell yourself that you can "fix it in post-production" or "I can edit that out." Perhaps you can. It is usually easier, however, to just shoot it right in first place. Sometimes, 10 seconds of work when you shoot can save you an hour or more in the editing room. So remember; scout and scout again. Keep in mind the rules of composition and have fun shooting.

Lighting

For many, the Dutch masters like Jan Vermeer, Gerrit Honthorst, Frans Hals and, of course, Rembrandt, are among the greatest painters to ever grace the canvas with a brush. Part of their fame is their ability capture life and intimacy with a glazing that is yet to be matched. But what truly sets them apart from their predecessors, is their masterful use of light.

There is a truth given to us in Vermeer's "The Milkmaid." The lonely stout maid of the house looks both tired and resolute in her work as she prepares a bit of bread and transfers milk from an urn to a bowl. There is wisdom and humility in her face; both youth and strength are dignified in her aging arms as she goes forth with her household duties. Yet on its own the painting would be nothing if not for Vermeer's use of the warm sunlight that cascades through the window. The soft light that gently caresses its way from her right cheek to the darkness of her left, sets this work apart from the hordes of mediocrity that was being churned out in the mid 17th century. The light is what dignifies this timeless work. This light was not accidental. The well-lit room was chosen for its light and Vermeer loved his room. Many of his works contain this same window and same light. The maid is doing kitchen work in a studio in the upper quarters of the home that doubled as the workspace to the great master painter. Simply put, this work was staged. If it were painted in the kitchen, the light would not have been this angelic. Vermeer had the tools of a household worker brought to the third floor so that he could paint it.

Photography, like the Dutch paintings, thrives on planning, scouting, and most importantly, light. Exceptional lighting can make an otherwise boring image into one that is cherished. Most photographers, painters, film makers, and artists will tell you that lighting is the key to a successful image. What they won't tell you is that beautiful light is not quite as complex or as difficult as it would first appear. Like composition, there are a few tricks and rules that make lighting your photograph simple.

Quality of Light

Different types of light have different effects in photography. We call these attributes the quality of light. Some qualities that light can have are direct or reflected, hard or soft; light can be bright or dim, and it can have different color temperatures, like warm or cool. All of these attributes, or qualities, come together to create the lighting in your photograph. Sometimes you will be in control of the lighting; sometimes you will have no control at all. Most of the time you will have partial control over the light that you are working with. Making minor changes can have a profound effect.

Hard and Soft Light

Have you ever noticed how evenly lit, shadow free, and soft subjects look when they stand by a window with indirect light shining through the panes? This is a great example of soft lighting. There are relatively few shadows and the light appears to fade smoothly as it wraps around corners. Compare that scene to a dark basement or garage, lit only with a bare 60w bulb. The light casts hard shadows on the wall. The eyes of your subject look sunken in and your subject's nose casts a deep shadow across his face. This is hard lighting.

The larger your light source is, the softer your light will be. The flash on your camera is a small light source, so it is a relatively hard light. Certainly the sun is the largest and brightest light source that we have, but because it is so far away its apparent size is quite small; thus the sun is another good example of hard lighting; but when it is overcast, the clouds scatter the hard light from the sun, and the light becomes very soft. Just as the clouds modify the light from the sun to make it soft, almost all light can be modified.

The Sun or Natural Light

We owe our life to it. Without it, our planet would be lifeless and cold. Yet, for a photographer, the sun presents several challenges. Because it is so bright and so small in the sky, it cast very hard shadows, especially when directly overhead. At noon, the sun has less atmosphere to travel through, and therefore is even more harsh than at dusk. Beyond that, when it's overhead, it casts hard shadows directly down on your subjects' faces; it can make their eyes look sunken, wrinkles look more dramatic, and colors can look washed out. On top of that, the sun is constantly moving, or rather we're moving in relation to the sun, so the light is never the same. But the sun can also produce beautiful light. As if we are all predisposition to love the sun, entire cities can literally stop in their track if the sunset is just right. There are times when no man-made light create beauty in a scene the way the sun can. Knowing how to use the sun is an art and a gift -- and no secret.

People look their best when the sun is no higher than about 45 degrees above the horizon. Shooting at the "golden hour" or about 30 minutes before and after sunset or sunrise can make a boring landscape look as if it were painted with golden pigments by God himself. The grays and whites come alive with colors that the best cameras, painters, and poets could only pretend to mimic at best.

But photographic moments don't always happen when the lighting is perfect. If you have to shoot at noon, you will have to compensate. Tell your camera to use its flash, which will help to fill in the shadows and make your subject pop out from the background. This will also work if your subject is backlit or side lit by the sun or any other light source.

Remember color temperature from the end of chapter 3. Your camera's flash puts out light at 6,000 K. The sun can range from 2,500 K or so at sunset to more than 6,000 K at noon. If you use your flash at sunset, you are now using mixed light. If you color balance your camera for the flash, the sunlight will look even more orange. If you correct for the sun, the flash will look blue. Perhaps an orange sunset is what you want. If not, you can put color corrective lenses called gels on your flash. If you use a warming gel (such as CTO, color temperature orange, or perhaps a 1/2 CTO), this will make the light emitting from the flash the same or at least a similar color to the warm sunset. Then the light from the flash and the light from the sun will be relatively the same color temperature.

Another method of compensating for the hard light of sun is to use a reflector to bounce sunlight into your shadow areas. This will keep your subjects from looking underexposed in some places, and overexposed in other places. You can buy these at your local photographic store, or you can make one yourself with a car windshield sun blocker or even cardboard spray painted silver. You can also move your subject into the shade of a tree or ramada, and still use a reflector or fill flash.

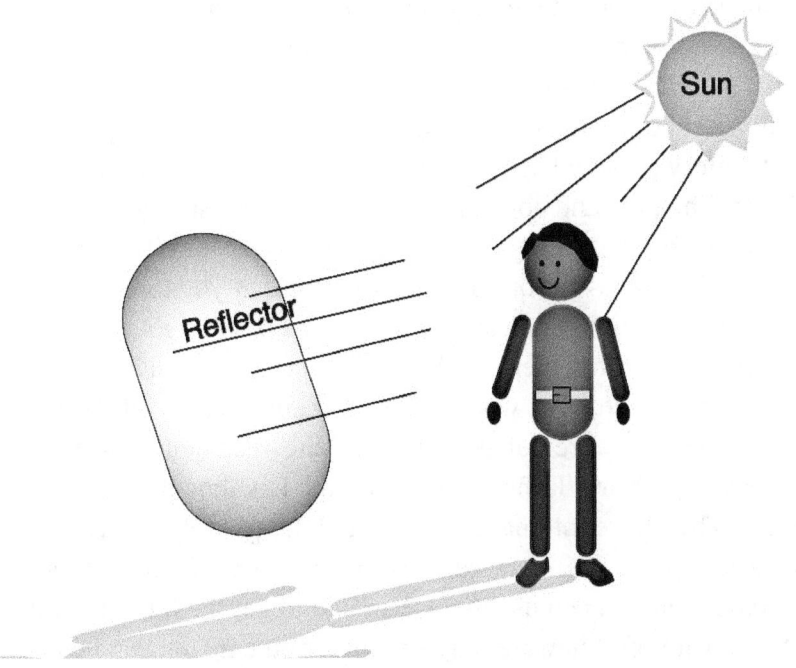

On an overcast day, the sun will not produce hard light, because the clouds will defuse and soften the sunlight. This happens because the sunlight hits the clouds and scatters; the clouds then have a "glowing effect." In reality, the clouds are now your light source; they have the appearance of being much larger than the sun, so the light is softer. This type of natural light is cooler in color temperature than the sun. It's also not as bright. This means that if you are using a fill light, you won't need as much power from your artificial light source to attain the same effect. Also because the light is softer, a reflector may not be as dramatic as it is with direct sunlight -- although it will still do something.

Artificial Lighting

Of course, the sun is not the only light source that we have. Artificial light, or light that is not from the sun, comes with its own challenges and advantages. With sunlight you get what you get, and it's constantly changing. With man-made light you have more control and more consistency. When it comes to photography, there are two types of artificial light, continuous and strobe. Continuous lighting stays on all the time, while strobes are on for just a fraction of a second. The flash on your camera is one type of strobe, and it's probably the one you will use the most.

When it comes to artificial lighting, you have choices; there are small battery powered speed lights, studio strobes, or continuous lighting. The pros and cons of each are worth considering, but the techniques for controlling and using all three are almost identical.

The advantages to continuous lights are that you don't have to use a remote trigger. You can see the effects of the light as you set them up and position them; and you can use continuous lights for motion picture setups as well. The disadvantages are that they produce heat, they are not as bright, and they use more power.

Speed lights are flashes that fit into the hot shoe on your camera. They have internal batteries, and many of them have auto exposure capabilities. They can also be taken off of your camera with ease, and you can use more than one to get the lighting effect that you want; but they are only on for a moment so it can be hard to tell what the lighting looks like while you are setting up. Speed lights also have limited power output capabilities. Most of the time, however, they do produce more than enough light to work with.

Studio strobes, on the other hand, can produce a lot of light. Though they are only on for moment, they do have modeling lights so that you can see what you are doing while you create your setup. On the downside, they are bulky and they have to be plugged into a power source, like a wall outlet, a generator, or an external battery pack. The principles of lighting your set with studio strobes, continuous lights, or speed lights are almost identical, and many times these lights are interchangeable.

TTL

There are many advantages to having a powerful flash right on your camera. It's highly portable and powerful, it snaps into place right on top of your camera, and it chooses its power output automatically via TTL or *Through The Lens Metering*. With TTL your flash will communicate with your camera, and together they decide how much power to produce. Most of the time this is good. Just like using TTL auto exposure without a flash, TTL with a flash is fast, convenient, and simple to use; but again there are some things that can cause your camera and flash to get confused. When the subject, or background, of your photograph are much darker or lighter than middle gray, your camera will misunderstand what it is exposing for and your image will likely become under or overexposed.

You already know that you can tell your camera to correct its exposure by adjusting the auto exposure bias. You can also correct for this with the flash power exposure bias. You will have to read your owner's manual to find out how to do this on your camera. On my camera, it can be adjusted both in the camera and on the flash.

One of my favorite things to do when shooting outdoors is to tell my camera to underexpose by about one stop and also tell my flash to overexpose by about one stop. The net result is that my subjects have proper exposure and sky and background are underexposed by about one stop. This introduces drama and adds a level of impact that the photograph otherwise would not have.

Automatic TTL and automatic TTL with exposure bias adjustment are not the only way to shoot. Sometimes they're not even the best way to shoot. All of the exposure decisions can be made by you with manual settings. Learning to use your flash in manual mode is a must for anyone serious about lighting. Automatic TTL is a powerful tool and I rely on it often, but no computer can calculate art. Using your flash in manual mode will help you understand why your camera makes the exposure choices that it does. Knowing this will make you better at using Automatic TTL with exposure compensation. Don't be afraid to play with these settings. In this digital world, you are not wasting any film; the results of experimentation are instant, and you will know right away what works and what does not.

Modify The Light

Adjusting the way your flash creates and directs its light is a great way to keep your photographs looking fresh. Another thing you can do to make your on-camera flash more interesting is to bounce it off of a wall or the ceiling. Having a flash on your camera is nice, but this light comes directly from your camera, bounces off of your subject, and comes directly back to your camera. The result is that your image can have a flat look, especially if the flash makes up the majority of the light required to make your image. If you turn the flash up or to the side, the bounced light will be defused, softer, and not so direct. (If you are using the built-in flash from your camera, you probably will not be able to do this; it will most likely have to be a flash that fits onto your camera's hot shoe.)

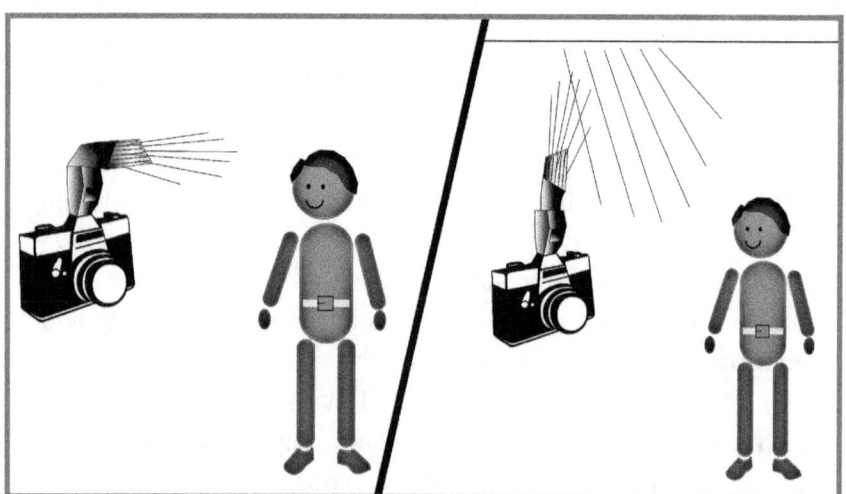

Along with bouncing your flash off of the ceiling or walls, there are several tools that are sold at your local photography shop that modify the way the light comes out of your flash. Some of them defuse the light, some bounce it. It is worth taking the time to check into what some of these modifiers do. I keep several kinds in my bag. One of my go-to defusers is a little foggy white box that attaches to the top the flash. This helps to defuse the light so that some of it scatters around the room and some of it is directed at my subject; it also makes the light source just a little bit larger. It only costs about $15 -- not a bad price to soften the quality of a strobe.

Off-Camera Flash

One of the best ways to keep your image from having that flat look that can come from the on-camera flash is to take the flash off of your camera. You can even add more than one flash to your system, and this does not have to cost a fortune. There are several speed lights on the market that do not have TTL. They are usually off brand gear, but they work great, and you can pick them up cheap. If you want to get into a multi-light set up, this can be good way to go.

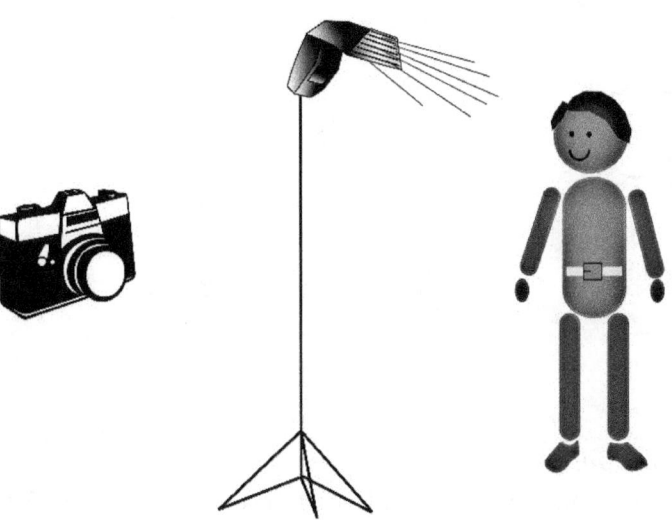

When you move your flash off of your camera, you gain the option to use soft boxes and umbrellas that would otherwise be too large to use while the flash is on your camera. Flashes have a small light source, so the light is naturally hard. By using an umbrella and an off-camera flash on a light stand, your light will be softer and very adjustable. You also have the freedom to add more flashes. Most setups are 1 to 4 flashes but from time to time, people do use more. If you know your way around your camera and you want to play with some more complex flash setups, I would recommend having at least two flashes on some stands with umbrellas. You will also want a wireless trigger set up as well. Some are already built into your camera and flash; some are after-market. Check your camera's manual or ask your local camera shop about this. No matter what method you used, you will need a way to trigger your flash when it is off of your cameras hot shoe.

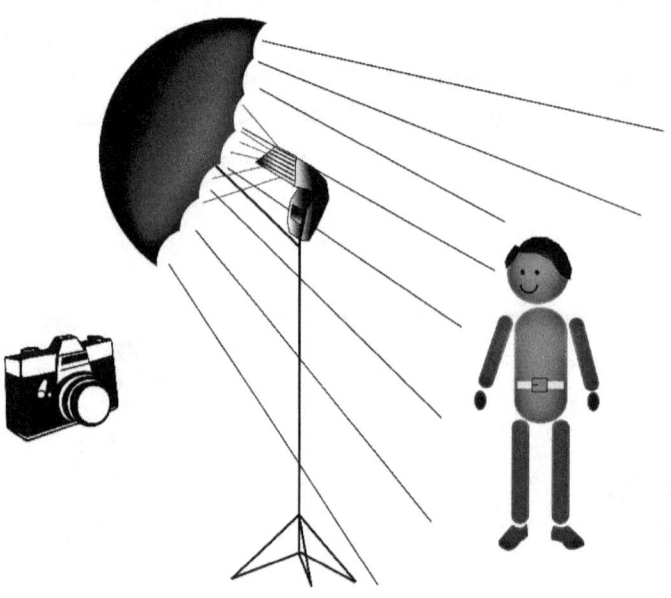

Multiple Lights

While it is possible to create fine lighting with just one light, having a few more lights can help you to fine tune your image. This may sound like a tricky thing to do, and it can be. Remember to go slow and add lights one at a time. Don't just jump into a ten light set up. Start with one, and then go to two and so on. If something looks wrong, test each light one at a time to see where the problem is.

Key Light

All lights have names so that we can tell them apart. The primary light is the *key*. This is normally the brightest. In the previous image the key is a strobe with an umbrella to defuse and soften the reflected light; there is no other light used. Normally, the next light someone might add to a set up is the fill light.

Fill Light

Fill lights fill in the shadows caused by the key and provide more even lighting throughout your photograph. You can create a fill light with a key and a reflector, or for more control you can use two lights. You can also use the sun as your key light and a strobe or reflector as a fill light.

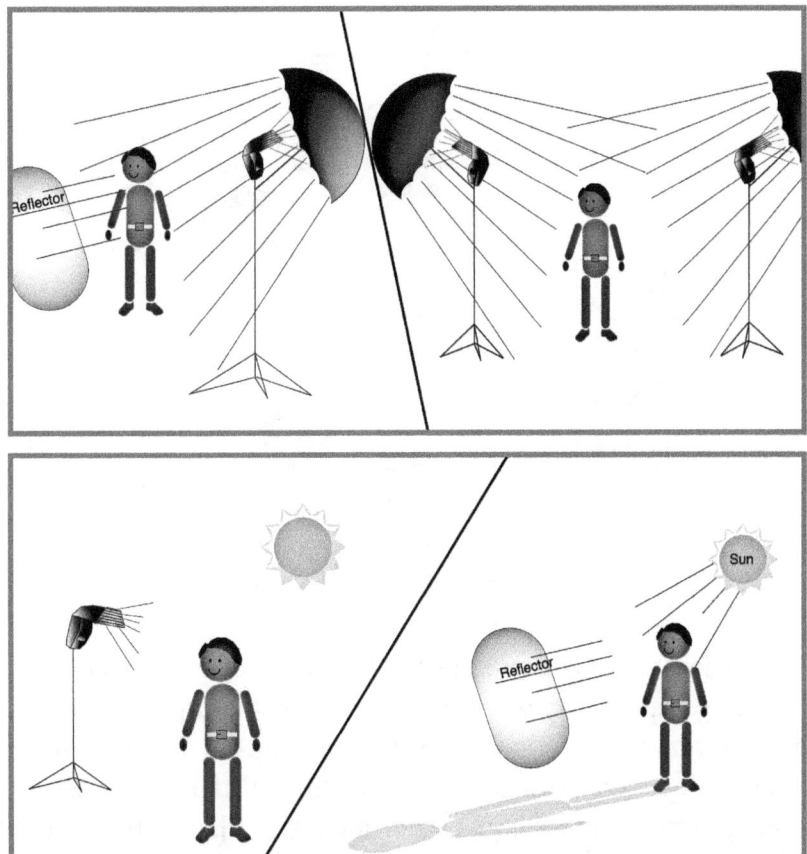

54
Four Light Set Up

Although we can do a lot with just two lights, below is a top-down view example of a common four light set up. The key light is your primary light. All of the other lights will have their power output based on the brightness of the key. The key can be positioned in several places. Here we have it at about 45 degrees from the camera. The fill light is about half the power (for a 2 to 1 ratio), and is on the opposite side of the camera. The backlight is normally a similar power to the fill but could be brighter or dimmer. It helps separate your subject from its background. The background light keeps the background lit and can be used to make the background more interesting. It is whatever power it needs to be to gain the desired effect.

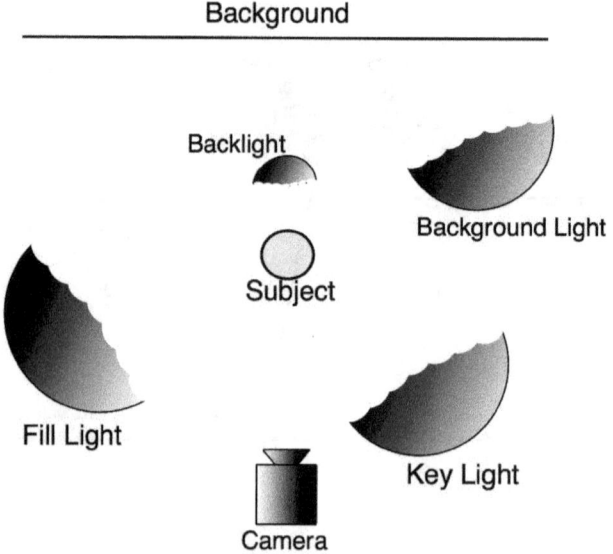

You don't need a set up this big to get professional results, but it is always fun to play with new tricks. This four light configuration is a time honored set up in both still and motion picture production. You have no obligation to stick with these lighting formats; they are just a starting point. Play with your lights and have fun. Don't be afraid to try new things. All of this takes time to learn, and practice is important. If you find something you like better, go with that. Lighting is not only a science, but also an art.

I know lights can be expensive but they don't have to be. It took me a while before I started lighting my sets with professional equipment. When I was in film school we used work lamps from the hardware store. These lights had small mettle scoops, a built in clamp, and used regular lightbulbs. They only cost about $8 each and did a good job. Their light could then be defused by bouncing it off of some white poster board, or using a translucent shower curtain to create a soft box. I have also seen pro-photographers, use all of kinds of creative things to light a room. Even though these tools are often quick and cheap, the results look professional. Though there are many rules to lighting, rules were made to be broken. Feel free to experiment, and try new things.

Final Thoughts

Over the years, photography has brought me great joy. It has encouraged me to look at the world through different lenses. It has enticed me to go to places I would not have otherwise gone. I'm not a morning person, but you have to get up early to capture that morning light. Without that prod, I would have just stayed in bed, or my sleeping bag, and I would have missed some of the most beautiful views the world has to offer. I owe a lot to my cameras, and I have learned a lot from them. But to learn anything from them I first had to learn how to use them. Using a camera is both a science and an art, left brain and right, and it's mentally and physically taxing. At the end of a long wedding, both my body and mind are exhausted. After the wedding, I wait a few days and then review the photos on my computer. It is a lot like Christmas: "What did I get?" But none of the stunning images in my portfolio would have been possible without tens of thousands of really bad ones. Even today, I will shoot a wedding and capture 3,000 or so shots. I only deliver about 300. Thats a 10 to 1 shot ratio. I'm not saying that the other 9 are bad. Many times I have 5 versions of the same shot, and only one is best. So the others get shelved. Ansel Adams said, "Twelve significant photographs in one year is a good crop." He is right. It takes many bad photographs to make a good one and most good ones will never be great. My first photographs were simply terrible.

What is it, though, that Ansel Adams had that made his photographs significant? What makes an image great? Certainly the rules of art come together to make a great image, but what about those great photos that break all the rules? How can those be great as well? A photograph can be well lit, well composed, well shot -- everything about it can be perfect, but if it does not *impact* the viewer, it's worthless. Those photographs that by every other standard should be junk, yet everyone seems to love, have impact.

The rules of photography and art can help you create impact, but only *you* can really make it happen. I can tell you from experience, the photos that have it are not always the ones you think will be great when you click the shutter. Occasionally, it's those shots you initially disregarded that end up being the best.

Sometimes, I still pull out those old photos that I took as a child. My parents were generous with their film budget, and there is truly not a decent photograph anywhere in the mix. They would impact no one. But I enjoyed shooting. I still remember that sound -- a combination of a click and ping as the cheap spring opened and then closed the plastic shutter, followed by the zipper-like winding noise as my thumb hastily advanced the reel to the next frame so that I could blow yet another shot. It was one of the many sounds of summer. It was fun. In the following years, I would graduate to a 35mm SLR and shoot black and white film for classes, fun, and sometimes for family members who wanted portraits. My point? I have taken more bad photographs than most people will shoot in their entire lives.

Don't be afraid to burn through frames and keep that shutter moving; don't be afraid to shoot junk images. You paid a lot of money for your camera, and its shutter is good for at least 150,000 shots, and in some cases, much more. I encourage you to wear your camera out. But don't just shoot for the sake of shooting. Keep the science of the camera in your mind as you work. Your camera has a setting to auto display a preview image after each shot. Turn it on. Check the preview screen on your camera often. If you don't like something about your image, ask yourself, "What caused this?" Is it a composition problem or technical one?

Get a good handle on reciprocity, depth of field, color balance, and lighting. These things just take practice. If you don't have a tripod, get one. Remember that the science and the camera gear are just half the equation. Keep the rules of art in mind. Remember the Rule of Thirds, leading looks, balance, leading lines, and backgrounds. Working both sides of the brain like this can be hard and it can wear you out, but it's worth it.

Keep some tools in your camera bag. Along with my normal camera gear, I have a multitool with pliers and a knife in my bag; I also keep a flashlight, extra batteries, gaffer's tape, clamps,

Sharpies and pens, extra memory cards, camera cleaning supplies, a handkerchief, and perhaps most importantly, a granola bar. It's hard to shoot when you're thinking about food.

One of the most important things you can do as a photographer is to find a hero. I don't mean Bat Man, though I'm sure he has some cool toys to play with. I mean find some other photographer whose work you identify with. Their work should impact you. I have several, and not all of them are photographers. I love the Dutch master painters and I often try to use their examples of light in my work. It's a challenge to make light look that good, but it's not impossible. Who is your hero? You can see my work at www.JasonYoun.com. I'm not saying I need to be your hero, but I can't write this entire book and not plug my work just once.

Years ago, I earned a pilot's license. Right after my check ride an old pilot named Roy came up to me and congratulated me. Roy has tens of thousands of hours in the sky and in 2004 he was inducted into the hall of fame at the *Pima Air & Space Museum* in Tucson, Arizona. He is literally a living legend, so his words bear a certain weight. He said one thing that has stuck with me: "Now you have a license to learn."

Keep in mind that photography is a learning experience. Never stop learning new things or trying new techniques. Most of all, keep shooting.

Please take the time to give this book a review on line.

Thank you for reading my first book, a longer more in depth version, *Mastering Digital Photography: Jason Youn's Essential Guide to Understanding the Art & Science of Aperture, Shutter, Exposure, Light, & Composition* is available for both Kindle and paperback! This new book greatly expands on all of the information found here, and it includes a detailed tips and tricks section to help you on your way.

Enjoy your camera and keep shooting!

www.ingramcontent.com/pod-product-compliance
Lightning Source LLC
Chambersburg PA
CBHW071637170526
45166CB00003B/1355